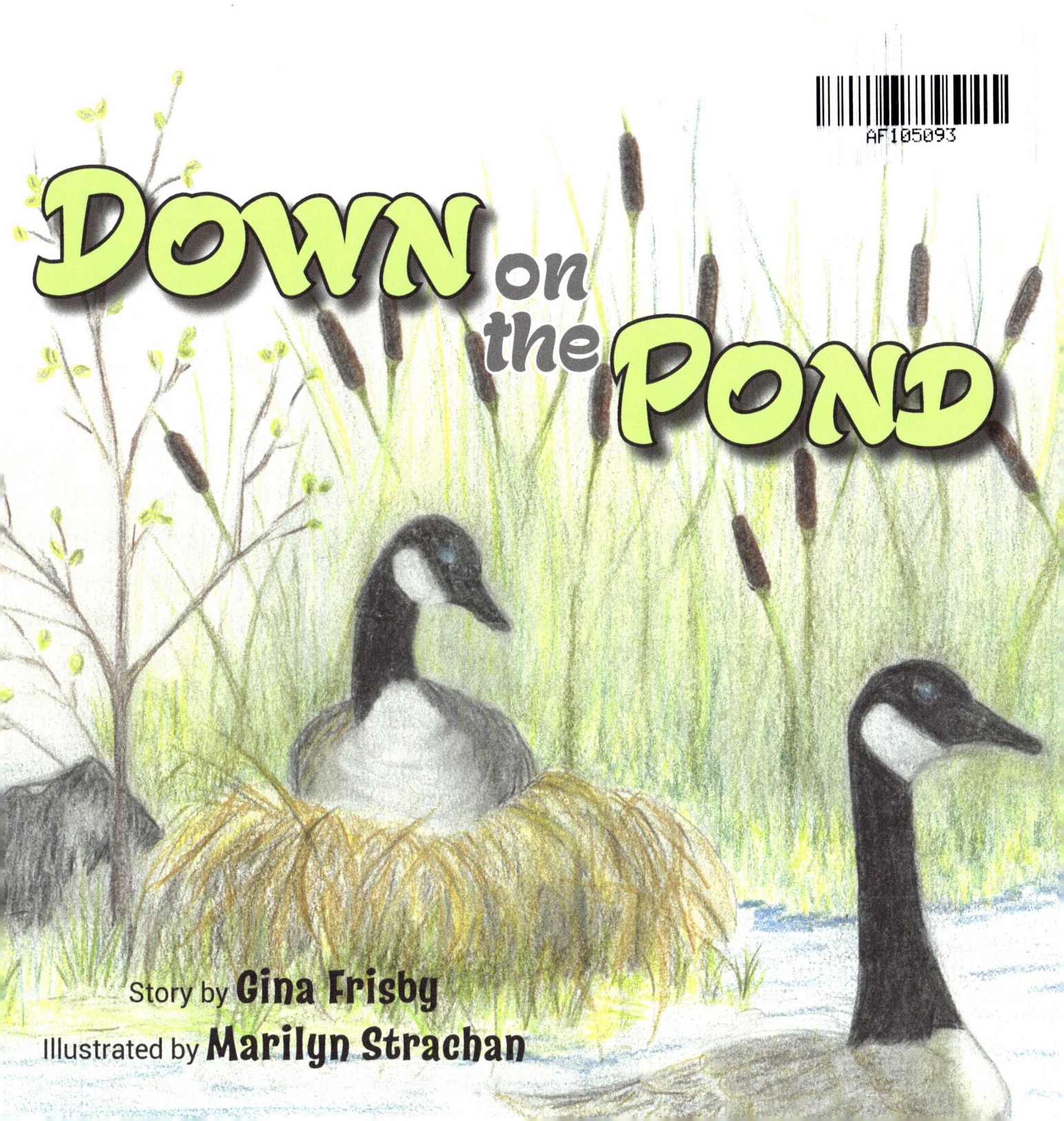

Down on the Pond
Copyright © 2020 by Gina Frisby
Illustrations by Marilyn Strachan

All rights reserved. No part of this publication may be reproduced, distributed, or transmitted in any form or by any means, including photocopying, recording, or other electronic or mechanical methods, without the prior written permission of the author, except in the case of brief quotations embodied in critical reviews and certain other non-commercial uses permitted by copyright law.

Tellwell Talent
www.tellwell.ca

ISBN
978-0-2288-3565-3 (Hardcover)
978-0-2288-3564-6 (Paperback)
978-0-2288-4140-1 (eBook)

GINA FRISBY
MARILYN STRACHAN

Dedication

For Sophia and Alden
who love the adventures
down on the pond
as much as I do...

Down on the pond

Where the wildflowers grow

Lives a small group of animals

Waiting for spring to show.

Down on the pond

A pair of geese stay

One on the nest

And one to survey.

As night quickly approaches

Papa takes a turn on the nest

So Mama can feed

And have a much needed rest.

Tomorrow is here!

Oh, what a day

The celebration of life

Is well underway.

Mama has her goslings

Settled down for the night

Can't wait for daybreak

To show them off right.

What a celebration they'll have

Meeting all the new folks

Showing off their new family

In the first few strokes.

The beaver is first

To meet the new chicks

He guards the new family

As he chews on his sticks.

The ducks are excited

The new brood is here

They hear little peeps

But know to stay clear.

The deer hover close

At the edge of the water

They have their first glimpse

Of the young with their father.

The great blue heron

Standing proudly at the shore

Watching with interest

Five chicks not four

It's their first swim

In a joyful parade

Across to the limb

And so not afraid.

Up on the log

Basking in the sun

The family is present

And all having fun.

A celebration of life

A strong solid bond

Can't wait for what's next

Down on the pond.

About the Author

Gina Frisby lives in Quesnel, British Columbia on acreage featuring a gorgeous pond with a walking trail. It is here that she finds inspiration to write her stories. Gina and her family love to spend time walking the pond and watching the animals. She believes every animal has a personality and hopes she reflects that in her stories.

Reading has always been a passion for Gina. She loves to pass on her love of books to others, especially children. There is something to be said about opening up a child's imagination. It's special. Magical!

www.ingramcontent.com/pod-product-compliance
Lightning Source LLC
LaVergne TN
LVHW072114060526
838200LV00061B/4891